LIVE *inspired*

GRATITUDE JOURNAL

WITH *Farin Doran*

CHECK OUT

FARINDORAN.COM/LIVE-INSPIRED

for additional free resources and access to
the live inspired community.

First Edition

ISBN: 978-0-578-85519-6

Design by Margaret Cogswell
www.margaretcogswell.com

THIS BOOK IS DEDICATED TO

YOU.

Not the girl behind you or next to you, not the girl on the Internet with 1.6M followers, not the girl from your high school ... This book is dedicated to you, the one who is holding this book in her hands and who has every intention of living life on purpose and with gratitude.

The fact that you even picked this book up and decided to dive in means that you, my friend, are preparing yourself to live your best life.

So girl, let's get inspired, let's cultivate some gratitude, and let's do this together. You are the star!

LET TODAY
BE THE
START OF
SOMETHING
new

Welcome

to the beginning of the next 100 days of your life. In this gratitude journal we are going to take it day by day and celebrate the things that you are grateful for.

WHY Gratitude?

For the last 30 plus years of my life, I have learned that the only thing CERTAIN about life is that there is uncertainty in each day. What does that mean? It means that the only thing we can be sure about is that each day can be different; there are no two days exactly the same. Life can change, things can happen, and good things can happen just as frequently as bad. One day you are sitting on a beach, looking into the eyes of your loved one, saying "My life is so perfect right now," and the next you are crying in a closet about your pants not fitting!

So, how do we keep the happiness? How do we keep a positive mindset? How do we encourage ourselves to stay in a peaceful state?

Gratitude.

You have to find the things in life that you are grateful for. This journal is going to give you the opportunity to find things in your life that you are grateful for. You are going to find a minimum of three things each day that you can say “I am grateful for ___.” Yes, you will have rough days. Yes, there will be days you will say, “I legit have nothing to be grateful for today.” But those are the days that you need this journal more than ever. Those are the days that you pick up your pen, find a quiet spot, and reflect on what it is that you are GRATEFUL for.

BUT WAIT... *There's More!*

Don't you just love when they say that ^ on infomercials? You get all excited about one thing and then suddenly they sweeten the deal and make it even more exciting?

So, let's up this challenge and make it even better.

Not only are you going to write out your gratitude for the day ---

But also write out your intentions.

To have a life of purpose, you have to be intentional. What do you want to accomplish? What do you want the day to look like? If your intentions are to lay around and watch chick flicks while drinking mimosas all day, girl, write that down and do it! Do the things YOU want to do.

Lastly, but most importantly, we are going to incorporate the 3 M's.
Just you wait, more on that to come.
I promise, it will be good!

HOW DOES *this work?*

You, my friend, are in charge here. It is your responsibility to put this journal in a spot where you see it daily. It should be your constant reminder that you have to write in it. You owe it not only to yourself but to the journal. Don't leave it empty, give it what it wants, give it gratitude.

So every day, for 100 days, I want you to commit to taking a short moment out of your day to say what you are grateful for. I personally believe that starting your day with gratitude is an amazing practice. I think there is so much power in starting your day with a positive mindset, so no matter what happens that day, you knew that you had something to be thankful for.

Let's say you forget -- you run out the door and forget to write it down, or let's say mornings aren't your jam. Night time it is! Before you go to sleep, pick up your journal, write what you are grateful for, and go to bed happy. I guarantee you will start the next day a little better than the last.

What if I have nothing to be GRATEFUL *for one day?*

I would be lying if I said I haven't felt that way before. We all do. Again, this is when you need this journal the most. This is when you have to dig deep. This is the big challenge, and girl, you may have a lot of these challenges over the next 100 days. That is OK. Maybe you had a flat tire on the way to work, you were late, you missed an important meeting, and you sat in your car crying, waiting for the tow truck. Rough day ... I get it. Except, let's think what we CAN be grateful for instead. Grateful I had a job to drive to. Grateful I had insurance to help with the tow truck. Grateful for now being home safe with this journal in my hand ... see the trend here?

This will be your challenge and this is exactly why this matters. It matters that you look towards positivity in your day. Looking for something positive changes your whole perspective in your daily life. It almost forces you to see the brighter side of things. This will help you be the person that looks for the silver lining. This will help you to be happier, to have a smile on your face, and to ultimately change your life. And eventually it will be a habit for you; anytime something negative is going on, your mind will go towards something positive. Because you have been practicing for these moments daily.

If every day for 100 days, you found something that made your life worthwhile, made you smile, made you happy, and gave you the warm and fuzzies, then your brain will now be programmed to always look for the happiness and the warm and fuzzies.

I don't want you to just have gratitude here. My goal is for you to be happy. We may have never even met before but, girlfriend, I know that I 100% want YOU to be happy. Happy people make an amazing life and change the world. I'm counting on that from you!

The 3 M'S

These are the three things I want you to commit to daily to help you live your best life, to get motivated and to live inspired. You are going to check off the boxes for each thing you do. Seriously, how satisfying is it checking off a box, knowing that you accomplished those things for the day?

1. MAKE YOUR BED:

This is one of those things that you know you should do. You have probably heard this thousands of times from your parents growing up ... but here we are. We are back.

One of my favorite speeches I have ever heard came from Admiral William H. McRaven when he said:

"If you make your bed every morning you will have accomplished the first task of the day. It will give you a small sense of pride and it will encourage you to do another task and another and another ... And, if by chance you have a miserable day, you will come home to a bed that is made - that you made - and a made bed gives you encouragement that tomorrow will be better."

Imagine that. Imagine just one, tiny, small task that takes you less than a minute a day (unless you are the girl that has 35 oversized throw pillows on your bed that are only there for decoration ... then we will give you two minutes.) But IMAGINE that this small task could actually change your day. It will. I promise. There are actually studies that have been done proving that people who make their bed are happier, feel more accomplished, and are more productive the rest of the day.

So, let's do it together, friends... Let's commit to making our bed.

2. MOVE YOUR BODY:

Before you throw this book down and say, "Nope, not for me," hear me out. I am not telling you that you have to go for a run. I am not saying you need to sign up for CrossFit, and I am definitely not saying you need to do anything strenuous or crazy. I am simply telling you that you should move your body in some shape or form once a day. Physical activity releases chemicals in your body called endorphins. These endorphins actually trigger a positive feeling in your body. My goal for you, over these next 100 days, is to live inspired, to live your best life, and that absolutely includes feeling good about you and being happy. So if moving your body one day looks like a gym day, great. But if another day your physical activity and "moving your body" means walking outside, still great. If it means that you get to this part of the journal and you forgot to move your body, and you then stand up and do 20 squats ... girl, that is STILL great! Mission accomplished. The journal is serving its purpose. Find a way to move your body once a day. Then check it off! I promise you that checking off that box will feel good.

3. MANIFEST YOUR GOALS:

Your goals, your dreams, and everything you want in life can absolutely happen. It is completely up to you. As you check off these boxes and you get to this particular box, I want you to visualize your goals, your dreams, and your passions. I want you to manifest what you want every single day! If you can believe it yourself, you can make it happen. What you focus on, you bring to reality. You want it, manifest it!

Here is the secret to this box. No one is in charge of how big or small your goals are but you. You are in control here. If your goal is to be the top in sales for your company, manifest it girl! Now, if your goal is to simply not hit snooze the next day, I want you to still manifest it. You are in charge of your goals and having a goal just means you want to do more for yourself in any way that means something to you. The point of this box is to get you to actually think about what you want and remind yourself that you CAN get there.

One of my favorite success stories is J.K. Rowling, the author of the *Harry Potter* series. She was poor, on welfare, and had been rejected a ton of times. However, she never gave up. She kept believing in herself and what she was passionate about. Now, over 500 million copies of *Harry Potter* have been sold, making it the all-time bestselling book series.

Imagine if she had stopped manifesting her goals, dreams, and passions?

You don't have to be the next J.K. Rowling. No one is asking you to. This journal is simply asking you to be the best version of you. Imagine it, manifest it, and check off the box.

LET'S GET *Personal*

So who the heck is this Farin chick and how do I know this will work? If I am going to ask you to trust me and I am going to expect you to pick up this book daily and open it with intention, you should probably know the person behind the book.

Deep breath.
In through your nose ... out through your mouth ... let's go.

I am sitting here at my computer and every single time I get a little lost for words, I look over at the framed picture of my kids. I always look to them for inspiration. They are my constant reminder to push forward and to be a role model. I know that if I want my future little clones to be amazing, inspiring, sweet adults that I, myself, have to be amazing, inspiring, and sweet.

When I look at this picture of my children and myself sitting together, all matching like we stepped out of a J.Crew magazine, it is always a reminder that I earned this moment. I worked hard to be in that picture and to be the mom I am now and the mom I wish I had.

This leads right into why gratitude is important to me, and I'll give you the scoop.

I grew up around negativity. I grew up around people who, when they were mad, they were mad for a while, a LOOONG while.

I grew up around people that didn't sit down and have family dinners unless the television was on. We didn't talk at dinner. We made sure we were quiet, our elbows were off the table and that there was a clear view for the man of the house to see the TV.

There was no opportunity to talk about your day, how you felt, or anything.

I didn't like that.

And I think I put that feeling in the back of my head and remembered it until this day because the second I had a family, it was family dinners, no television, and quality conversations.

I am going to be super honest with you. And I feel like I should because, again, you are the one with my book in your hand and I would love to be on this adventure WITH you ...

So imagine the family dinners but in life form ... basically that feeling all over again and again in different situations in my life. A lot of things flat out sucked growing up, but I always held onto the thought of, "There's something else good." I didn't know at the time that I was having specific gratitude for things, I just knew that in order to move forward, I had to focus on the positives in my life.

It just so happens that at the right time and place, I met the most amazing guy who also had a similar situation. You see, I am here to tell you that it doesn't matter if your parents were the most negative people, or always saw the cup half empty, or didn't exactly treat you the way you wanted to be treated. That doesn't matter anymore. What matters is what YOU do about it. What matters is that YOU move forward. You are NOT in control of what others do but you are in 100% complete control over what YOU do.

So when my husband and I had children, we made it a point to do the things for our children that we would have changed in our own upbringings. We made it a point to talk about gratitude as much as we could. Whenever my kids would complain about something I would stop them quickly and turn it around. How can we rephrase that but also be happy about a situation? How can we still find something to be grateful for?

The kids figured out pretty quickly that they can't be negative around Mom.

Yes, you are allowed to be upset. You are allowed to cry. You can feel sorry about it for a while but you HAVE to find a way to turn it around. You have to find something positive in every situation.

This all sounds great, but let's be real, you don't always remember to "have gratitude." Life happens, you get busy, and suddenly it's been 4 months, 16 days and 2 hours since you last said something you were grateful for. Oops.

My husband and I started implementing gratitude at dinner. Hey, you eat everyday, right? So it is an EASY reminder. Every night at dinner, my family goes around the table and each person says something they are grateful for. It doesn't matter what crappy thing happened that day, what stress came about, what anxiety, or what vegetables are on their plates that they absolutely hate. When we start talking about gratitude, everyone starts smiling. It changes the whole day. And gratitude is contagious. One person says they are grateful for something and everyone nods and agrees and it just keeps flowing.

Imagine that. Imagine focusing on the things that you are happy for instead of the things you are not. If you focused a part of your day on things that you are GRATEFUL for, imagine how that can continue to flow throughout your day and also into other people's day.

So while you are still getting to know me, here is what I want you to know. I wasn't dealt this amazing hand in life. There wasn't a trust fund, a family that stayed together, or the perfect life. I will never pretend like everything was rainbows and butterflies to get to where I am now, because that's not true. And I am willing to bet that you reading this have also had things in your life that have made you feel BLAH. Maybe they even made you question if you COULD keep going and do more for you. Maybe you even weren't sure you were grateful for anything at one point.

The thing is, girlfriend, you CAN do more. You can be the best version of you. You can live a life that is inspiring. You CAN be everything you have ever wanted to be. And through this journal you are going to work on doing just that, every single day.

You can do this, girl. I believe in you.

ON TO THE *Challenge...*

Wait ... what? A challenge? Yes, girl! I love a good challenge and I think it brings extra commitment to yourself. You are challenging YOU and showing up for you!

So not only are you going to commit to writing down what you are grateful for, you are going to commit to doing this for 100 days. This is the #100daysofgratitudechallenge. And when you start in this book and you flip to the first page, you are entering day 1 of the 100 days. If you can write down 100 days worth of gratitude, that means for just about ⅓ of the year, YOU committed to being grateful and YOU committed to you! This is YOUR journal and YOUR journey and we are going to start showing up for YOU.

Every challenge needs some good steps, right?

I am going to lay it out for you so there is no confusion here. I got ya, girl!

1. Put your journal in a place where you see it every single day. Your nightstand, your kitchen, or keep it in your purse. Anywhere that you are guaranteed to have full eye contact with it.

2. Each day, open up to the next page and write out your gratitude for the day, your intentions, and check off your 3 M's. Remember this is a NO STRESS process. This isn't here to make you anxious or make you feel like you didn't do what you should, but to encourage

you to do more for you, put yourself first, and feel inspired.

3. For extra accountability and to make this more exciting, announce your challenge online. If you have a social media account, tag @liveinspiredjournal and use the hashtag #100daysofgratitudechallenge and #liveinspiredjournal. Each day, when you complete another day of the challenge and when you see a quote that speaks to you, snap a pic, share your journey and tag @liveinspiredjournal. My favorite part of doing anything inspiring and worthwhile is also inspiring others to do the same as well. We can do that together by sharing our journey!

4. Every 20 days, you are going to reflect on how far you have come. Why does this part matter? Because sometimes going into a 100 day challenge is overwhelming. We are not here to jump to the 100th step but rather to take each step at a time. So let's focus on getting to day 20, and then another 20, and then another, etc. On this reflection day, I want you to give yourself a happy dance, a high five, or pat yourself on the back, because you committed to showing up for YOU for a whole 20 days. For some, this will be the most they practiced gratitude for a whole year, so let's get excited about that!

5. Repeat. Do it again and again, and remember that practicing gratitude and taking these moments for yourself matters! You matter, your outlook on your life matters, your intentions matter, and your commitment matters!

SUPER PROUD OF YOU,

girlfriend!!!

FOLLOW *Me*

Farin Doran

@farindoran

Farin Doran

READY TO START YOUR GRATITUDE *journey?*

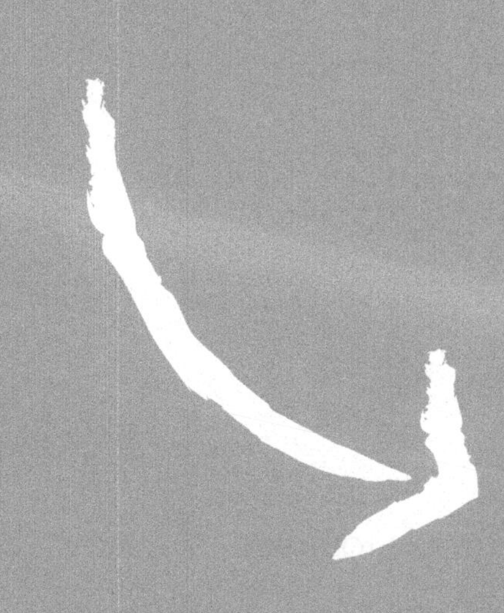

DATE ______________________

DAY ____ / 100

Act as if what you do makes a difference. It does. *William James*

TODAY I AM GRATEFUL FOR...

AND MY WINS WERE...

AND I COMPLETED THE 3 M'S

- [ ] MAKE YOUR BED.
- [ ] MOVE YOUR BODY.
- [ ] MANIFEST YOUR GOALS.

DATE ____________________

DAY ____ / 100

Success is not final, failure is not fatal: it is the courage to continue that counts.

Winston Churchill

TODAY I AM GRATEFUL FOR...

AND MY WINS WERE...

AND I COMPLETED THE 3 M'S

- [ ] MAKE YOUR BED.
- [ ] MOVE YOUR BODY.
- [ ] MANIFEST YOUR GOALS.

DATE ____________________

DAY ___ / 100

Never bend your head. Always hold it high. Look the world straight in the eye.

Helen Keller

TODAY I AM GRATEFUL FOR...

AND MY WINS WERE...

AND I COMPLETED THE 3 M'S

- [ ] MAKE YOUR BED.
- [ ] MOVE YOUR BODY.
- [ ] MANIFEST YOUR GOALS.

DATE ____________________

DAY ___ / 100

What you get by achieving your goals is not as important as what you become by achieving your goals. *Zig Ziglar*

TODAY I AM GRATEFUL FOR...

AND MY WINS WERE...

AND I COMPLETED THE 3 M'S

☐ MAKE YOUR BED. ☐ MOVE YOUR BODY. ☐ MANIFEST YOUR GOALS.

DATE ____________

DAY ___ / 100

Believe you can and you're halfway there.

Theodore Roosevelt

TODAY I AM GRATEFUL FOR...

AND MY WINS WERE...

AND I COMPLETED THE 3 M'S

- [ ] MAKE YOUR BED.
- [ ] MOVE YOUR BODY.
- [ ] MANIFEST YOUR GOALS.

DATE ____________________

DAY ___ / 100

When you have a dream, you've got to grab it and never let go. *Carol Burnett*

TODAY I AM GRATEFUL FOR...

AND MY WINS WERE...

AND I COMPLETED THE 3 M'S

- [ ] MAKE YOUR BED.
- [ ] MOVE YOUR BODY.
- [ ] MANIFEST YOUR GOALS.

DATE ______________________

DAY ___/ 100

I can't change the direction of the wind, but I can adjust my sails to always reach my destination. *Jimmy Dean*

TODAY I AM GRATEFUL FOR...

AND MY WINS WERE...

AND I COMPLETED THE 3 M'S

☐ MAKE YOUR BED. ☐ MOVE YOUR BODY. ☐ MANIFEST YOUR GOALS.

DATE ____________________

DAY ___ / 100

Life is like riding a bicycle. To keep your balance, you must keep moving.

Albert Einstein

TODAY I AM GRATEFUL FOR...

____

____

____

____

____

AND MY WINS WERE...

____

____

____

____

____

AND I COMPLETED THE 3 M'S

☐ MAKE YOUR BED. ☐ MOVE YOUR BODY. ☐ MANIFEST YOUR GOALS.

DATE ____________________

DAY ___ / 100

Just don't give up trying to do what you really want to do. Where there is love and inspiration, I don't think you can go wrong.

Ella Fitzgerald

TODAY I AM GRATEFUL FOR...

AND MY WINS WERE...

AND I COMPLETED THE 3 M'S

☐ MAKE YOUR BED. ☐ MOVE YOUR BODY. ☐ MANIFEST YOUR GOALS.

DATE ____________

DAY ___ / 100

You are never too old to set another goal or to dream a new dream. *C.S. Lewis*

TODAY I AM GRATEFUL FOR...

AND MY WINS WERE...

AND I COMPLETED THE 3 M'S

☐ MAKE YOUR BED. ☐ MOVE YOUR BODY. ☐ MANIFEST YOUR GOALS.

DATE ____________

DAY ___ / 100

You do not find the happy life. You make it.

Camilla Eyring Kimball

TODAY I AM GRATEFUL FOR...

AND MY WINS WERE...

AND I COMPLETED THE 3 M'S

☐ MAKE YOUR BED. ☐ MOVE YOUR BODY. ☐ MANIFEST YOUR GOALS.

DATE ____________________

DAY ___ / 100

It isn't where you came from. It's where you're going that counts. *Ella Fitzgerald*

TODAY I AM GRATEFUL FOR...

____

____

____

____

____

AND MY WINS WERE...

____

____

____

____

____

AND I COMPLETED THE 3 M'S

☐ MAKE YOUR BED. ☐ MOVE YOUR BODY. ☐ MANIFEST YOUR GOALS.

DATE ____________________

DAY ___ / 100

It is never too late to be what you might have been. *George Eliot*

TODAY I AM GRATEFUL FOR...

AND MY WINS WERE...

AND I COMPLETED THE 3 M'S

☐ MAKE YOUR BED. ☐ MOVE YOUR BODY. ☐ MANIFEST YOUR GOALS.

DATE ______________

DAY ___ / 100

Be the change that you wish to see in the world. *Mahatma Gandhi*

TODAY I AM GRATEFUL FOR...

AND MY WINS WERE...

AND I COMPLETED THE 3 M'S

- [ ] MAKE YOUR BED.
- [ ] MOVE YOUR BODY.
- [ ] MANIFEST YOUR GOALS.

DATE ____________

DAY ___ / 100

Let us make our future now, and let us make our dreams tomorrow's reality.

Malala Yousafzai

TODAY I AM GRATEFUL FOR...

____

____

____

____

____

AND MY WINS WERE...

____

____

____

____

____

AND I COMPLETED THE 3 M'S

- [ ] MAKE YOUR BED.
- [ ] MOVE YOUR BODY.
- [ ] MANIFEST YOUR GOALS.

DATE ____________________

DAY ___ / 100

If I cannot do great things, I can do small things in a great way.

Martin Luther King Jr.

TODAY I AM GRATEFUL FOR...

____

____

____

____

____

AND MY WINS WERE...

____

____

____

____

____

AND I COMPLETED THE 3 M'S

☐ MAKE YOUR BED. ☐ MOVE YOUR BODY. ☐ MANIFEST YOUR GOALS.

DATE ____________________

DAY ___ / 100

My mission in life is not merely to survive, but to thrive. *Maya Angelou*

TODAY I AM GRATEFUL FOR...

AND MY WINS WERE...

AND I COMPLETED THE 3 M'S

- [ ] MAKE YOUR BED.
- [ ] MOVE YOUR BODY.
- [ ] MANIFEST YOUR GOALS.

DATE ____________________

DAY ___ / 100

Each person must live their life as a model for others. *Rosa Parks*

TODAY I AM GRATEFUL FOR...

AND MY WINS WERE...

AND I COMPLETED THE 3 M'S

☐ MAKE YOUR BED. ☐ MOVE YOUR BODY. ☐ MANIFEST YOUR GOALS.

DATE ____________________

DAY ___/ 100

If we did the things we are capable of doing, we would literally astound ourselves.

Thomas Edison

TODAY I AM GRATEFUL FOR...

AND MY WINS WERE...

AND I COMPLETED THE 3 M'S

- [ ] MAKE YOUR BED.
- [ ] MOVE YOUR BODY.
- [ ] MANIFEST YOUR GOALS.

DATE ____________________

DAY ___ / 100

Always keep your eyes open. Keep watching. Because whatever you see can inspire you.

Grace Coddington

TODAY I AM GRATEFUL FOR...

AND MY WINS WERE...

AND I COMPLETED THE 3 M'S

- [ ] MAKE YOUR BED.
- [ ] MOVE YOUR BODY.
- [ ] MANIFEST YOUR GOALS.

STAY POSITIVE. FORGIVE OTHERS. INVEST IN YOURSELF. TRUST YOUR INSTINCTS. LEAD WITH AN OPEN HEART. DON'T LET OTHERS RUIN YOUR DAY. DO THINGS THAT BRING YOU JOY. BE OF SERVICE TO HUMANITY. FIND YOUR SOUL TRIBE. LOVE YOURSELF.

LEWIS *Howes*

Let's Reflect

The past 20 days, I am most proud of...

I want to be more intentional about...

I am going to keep going because...

DATE ____________________

DAY ____ / 100

If you want to live a happy life, tie it to a goal, not to people or objects.

Albert Einstein

TODAY I AM GRATEFUL FOR...

AND MY WINS WERE...

AND I COMPLETED THE 3 M'S

☐ MAKE YOUR BED. ☐ MOVE YOUR BODY. ☐ MANIFEST YOUR GOALS.

DATE ___________________

DAY ___ / 100

Never give up on a dream just because of the time it will take to accomplish it. The time will pass anyway. *Earl Nightingale*

TODAY I AM GRATEFUL FOR...

AND MY WINS WERE...

AND I COMPLETED THE 3 M'S

- [ ] MAKE YOUR BED.
- [ ] MOVE YOUR BODY.
- [ ] MANIFEST YOUR GOALS.

DATE ____________________

DAY ____/ 100

I never dream of success. I worked for it.

Estee Lauder

TODAY I AM GRATEFUL FOR...

AND MY WINS WERE...

AND I COMPLETED THE 3 M'S

☐ MAKE YOUR BED. ☐ MOVE YOUR BODY. ☐ MANIFEST YOUR GOALS.

DATE ____________________

DAY ___ / 100

I challenge you to make your life a masterpiece. I challenge you to join the ranks of those people who live what they teach, who walk their talk.

Tony Robbins

TODAY I AM GRATEFUL FOR...

AND MY WINS WERE...

AND I COMPLETED THE 3 M'S

- [ ] MAKE YOUR BED.
- [ ] MOVE YOUR BODY.
- [ ] MANIFEST YOUR GOALS.

DATE ____________________

DAY ___ / 100

Create the highest, grandest vision possible for your life, because you become what you believe. *Oprah Winfrey*

TODAY I AM GRATEFUL FOR...

AND MY WINS WERE...

AND I COMPLETED THE 3 M'S

- [ ] MAKE YOUR BED.
- [ ] MOVE YOUR BODY.
- [ ] MANIFEST YOUR GOALS.

DATE ____________

DAY ___ / 100

I didn't wait for people to come to me. I created opportunities for myself through my actions. *Melanie Mitro*

TODAY I AM GRATEFUL FOR...

AND MY WINS WERE...

AND I COMPLETED THE 3 M'S

☐ MAKE YOUR BED. ☐ MOVE YOUR BODY. ☐ MANIFEST YOUR GOALS.

DATE ______________________

DAY ___ / 100

Maybe, if you put your disbelief aside, roll up your sleeves, take some risks, and totally go for it, you'll wake up one day and realize you're living the kind of life you used to be jealous of.

Jen Sincero

TODAY I AM GRATEFUL FOR...

AND MY WINS WERE...

AND I COMPLETED THE 3 M'S

- [ ] MAKE YOUR BED.
- [ ] MOVE YOUR BODY.
- [ ] MANIFEST YOUR GOALS.

DATE ____________________

DAY ___/ 100

Show up in every single moment like you're meant to be there. *Marie Forleo*

TODAY I AM GRATEFUL FOR...

AND MY WINS WERE...

AND I COMPLETED THE 3 M'S

- [ ] MAKE YOUR BED.
- [ ] MOVE YOUR BODY.
- [ ] MANIFEST YOUR GOALS.

DATE ____________

DAY ___ / 100

Whatever it is that you think you want to do, and whatever it is that you think stands between you and that, stop making excuses. You can do anything. *Katia Beauchamp*

TODAY I AM GRATEFUL FOR...

AND MY WINS WERE...

AND I COMPLETED THE 3 M'S

- [ ] MAKE YOUR BED.
- [ ] MOVE YOUR BODY.
- [ ] MANIFEST YOUR GOALS.

DATE ____________________

DAY ___ / 100

Define success in your own terms, achieve it by your own rules, and build a life you're proud to live. *Anne Sweeney*

TODAY I AM GRATEFUL FOR...

AND MY WINS WERE...

AND I COMPLETED THE 3 M'S

- [ ] MAKE YOUR BED.
- [ ] MOVE YOUR BODY.
- [ ] MANIFEST YOUR GOALS.

DATE ______________

DAY ___ / 100

Believe that there are no limitations, no barriers to your success — you will be empowered and you will achieve.

Ursula Burns

TODAY I AM GRATEFUL FOR...

AND MY WINS WERE...

AND I COMPLETED THE 3 M'S

☐ MAKE YOUR BED. ☐ MOVE YOUR BODY. ☐ MANIFEST YOUR GOALS.

DATE ____________________

DAY ___ / 100

How wonderful it is that nobody need wait a single moment before starting to improve the world. *Anne Frank*

TODAY I AM GRATEFUL FOR...

AND MY WINS WERE...

AND I COMPLETED THE 3 M'S

- [ ] MAKE YOUR BED.
- [ ] MOVE YOUR BODY.
- [ ] MANIFEST YOUR GOALS.

DATE ______________

DAY ___ / 100

Surround yourself with the positive people, the people that are going to be lifting you up instead of bringing you down.

Ashley Kaskel

TODAY I AM GRATEFUL FOR...

AND MY WINS WERE...

AND I COMPLETED THE 3 M'S

- [ ] MAKE YOUR BED.
- [ ] MOVE YOUR BODY.
- [ ] MANIFEST YOUR GOALS.

DATE ______________

DAY ___ / 100

I've missed more than 9,000 shots in my career. I've lost almost 300 games. Twenty-six times, I've been trusted to take the game winning shot and missed. I've failed over and over and over again in my life. And that is why I succeed.

Michael Jordan

TODAY I AM GRATEFUL FOR...

____

____

____

____

____

AND MY WINS WERE...

____

____

____

____

____

AND I COMPLETED THE 3 M'S

☐ MAKE YOUR BED. ☐ MOVE YOUR BODY. ☐ MANIFEST YOUR GOALS.

DATE ____________________

DAY ____ / 100

The only difference between those of us who kinda push through and get there and those of us who don't, are some of us are willing to get our hands dirty and put the work in.

Alli Luchey

TODAY I AM GRATEFUL FOR...

AND MY WINS WERE...

AND I COMPLETED THE 3 M'S

- [ ] MAKE YOUR BED.
- [ ] MOVE YOUR BODY.
- [ ] MANIFEST YOUR GOALS.

DATE ____________________

DAY ____ / 100

One moment. One decision. One day at a time. That's what adds up to a brand new life. *Calie Calabrese*

TODAY I AM GRATEFUL FOR...

AND MY WINS WERE...

AND I COMPLETED THE 3 M'S

- [ ] MAKE YOUR BED.
- [ ] MOVE YOUR BODY.
- [ ] MANIFEST YOUR GOALS.

DATE ____________

DAY ___ / 100

It's not necessarily what happens to you but how you handle it. *Amanda Robinson*

TODAY I AM GRATEFUL FOR...

AND MY WINS WERE...

AND I COMPLETED THE 3 M'S

☐ MAKE YOUR BED. ☐ MOVE YOUR BODY. ☐ MANIFEST YOUR GOALS.

DATE ____________________

DAY ___ / 100

Your positive action combined with positive thinking results in success. *Shiv Khera*

TODAY I AM GRATEFUL FOR...

AND MY WINS WERE...

AND I COMPLETED THE 3 M'S

☐ MAKE YOUR BED. ☐ MOVE YOUR BODY. ☐ MANIFEST YOUR GOALS.

DATE ____________

DAY ___ / 100

You can't build a reputation on what you are going to do.

Henry Ford

TODAY I AM GRATEFUL FOR...

AND MY WINS WERE...

AND I COMPLETED THE 3 M'S

- [ ] MAKE YOUR BED.
- [ ] MOVE YOUR BODY.
- [ ] MANIFEST YOUR GOALS.

DATE ____________________

DAY ___ / 100

I am not a product of my circumstances, I am a product of my decisions.

Steven Covey

TODAY I AM GRATEFUL FOR...

AND MY WINS WERE...

AND I COMPLETED THE 3 M'S

☐ MAKE YOUR BED. ☐ MOVE YOUR BODY. ☐ MANIFEST YOUR GOALS.

WHEN
Gratitude
BECOMES
YOUR
DEFAULT
SETTING,
LIFE
CHANGES.

NANCY LEIGH *Demoss*

Let's Reflect

The past 20 days, I am most proud of...

I want to be more intentional about...

I am going to keep going because...

DATE ____________________

DAY ____ / 100

You will never be given a vision that you are not meant to pursue. *Lori Harder*

TODAY I AM GRATEFUL FOR...

AND MY WINS WERE...

AND I COMPLETED THE 3 M'S

- [ ] MAKE YOUR BED.
- [ ] MOVE YOUR BODY.
- [ ] MANIFEST YOUR GOALS.

DATE ____________________

DAY ___ / 100

Your level of success will rarely exceed your level of personal development, because success is something you attract by the person you become.

Hal Elrod

TODAY I AM GRATEFUL FOR...

AND MY WINS WERE...

AND I COMPLETED THE 3 M'S

- [ ] MAKE YOUR BED.
- [ ] MOVE YOUR BODY.
- [ ] MANIFEST YOUR GOALS.

DATE ______________

DAY ___ / 100

Change is often a silent job that requires patience and courage. Courage to be yourself. Courage to resist negativity. Courage to go beyond your boundaries. Courage to take responsibility for your own life.

Gordana Biernat

TODAY I AM GRATEFUL FOR...

AND MY WINS WERE...

AND I COMPLETED THE 3 M'S

- [ ] MAKE YOUR BED.
- [ ] MOVE YOUR BODY.
- [ ] MANIFEST YOUR GOALS.

DATE ____________________

DAY ___ / 100

If you cannot do great things, do small things in a great way. *Napoleon Hill*

TODAY I AM GRATEFUL FOR...

AND MY WINS WERE...

AND I COMPLETED THE 3 M'S

- [ ] MAKE YOUR BED.
- [ ] MOVE YOUR BODY.
- [ ] MANIFEST YOUR GOALS.

DATE ____________________

DAY ___ / 100

I've literally never looked back once I found that inner strength within me. We all have the ability to accomplish amazing things if we just took a chance on ourselves. *Melissa Bona*

TODAY I AM GRATEFUL FOR...

AND MY WINS WERE...

AND I COMPLETED THE 3 M'S

- [ ] MAKE YOUR BED.
- [ ] MOVE YOUR BODY.
- [ ] MANIFEST YOUR GOALS.

DATE ____________________

DAY ___ / 100

All our dreams can come true, if we have the courage to pursue them. *Walt Disney*

TODAY I AM GRATEFUL FOR...

AND MY WINS WERE...

AND I COMPLETED THE 3 M'S

- [ ] MAKE YOUR BED.
- [ ] MOVE YOUR BODY.
- [ ] MANIFEST YOUR GOALS.

DATE ____________________

DAY ___ / 100

The best time to plant a tree was 20 years ago. The second best time is now.

Chinese Proverb

TODAY I AM GRATEFUL FOR...

AND MY WINS WERE...

AND I COMPLETED THE 3 M'S

- [ ] MAKE YOUR BED.
- [ ] MOVE YOUR BODY.
- [ ] MANIFEST YOUR GOALS.

DATE ____________________

DAY ___ / 100

Do one thing every day that scares you.

Eleanor Roosevelt

TODAY I AM GRATEFUL FOR...

AND MY WINS WERE...

AND I COMPLETED THE 3 M'S

- [ ] MAKE YOUR BED.
- [ ] MOVE YOUR BODY.
- [ ] MANIFEST YOUR GOALS.

DATE ______________

DAY ___ / 100

Happiness is not something ready made. It comes from your own actions.

Dalai Lama XIV

TODAY I AM GRATEFUL FOR...

AND MY WINS WERE...

AND I COMPLETED THE 3 M'S

- [ ] MAKE YOUR BED.
- [ ] MOVE YOUR BODY.
- [ ] MANIFEST YOUR GOALS.

DATE ______________

DAY ____ / 100

Whatever you are, be a good one.

Abraham Lincoln

TODAY I AM GRATEFUL FOR...

AND MY WINS WERE...

AND I COMPLETED THE 3 M'S

- [ ] MAKE YOUR BED.
- [ ] MOVE YOUR BODY.
- [ ] MANIFEST YOUR GOALS.

DATE ____________________

DAY ___ / 100

Magic is believing in yourself. If you can make that happen, you can make anything happen. *Johann Wolfgang Von Goethe*

TODAY I AM GRATEFUL FOR...

AND MY WINS WERE...

AND I COMPLETED THE 3 M'S

☐ MAKE YOUR BED. ☐ MOVE YOUR BODY. ☐ MANIFEST YOUR GOALS.

DATE ____________________

DAY ___/ 100

If something is important enough, even if the odds are stacked against you, you should still do it. *Elon Musk*

TODAY I AM GRATEFUL FOR...

AND MY WINS WERE...

AND I COMPLETED THE 3 M'S

- [ ] MAKE YOUR BED.
- [ ] MOVE YOUR BODY.
- [ ] MANIFEST YOUR GOALS.

DATE ______________________

DAY ___ / 100

**We are what we repeatedly do.
Excellence, then, is not an act, but a habit.**

Aristotle

TODAY I AM GRATEFUL FOR...

AND MY WINS WERE...

AND I COMPLETED THE 3 M'S

☐ MAKE YOUR BED. ☐ MOVE YOUR BODY. ☐ MANIFEST YOUR GOALS.

DATE ____________________

DAY ___ / 100

Great things are done by a series of small things brought together.

Vincent Van Gogh

TODAY I AM GRATEFUL FOR...

AND MY WINS WERE...

AND I COMPLETED THE 3 M'S

- [ ] MAKE YOUR BED.
- [ ] MOVE YOUR BODY.
- [ ] MANIFEST YOUR GOALS.

DATE ______________________

DAY ___ / 100

The big secret in life is that there is no secret. Whatever your goal, you can get there if you're willing to work.

Oprah Winfrey

TODAY I AM GRATEFUL FOR...

AND MY WINS WERE...

AND I COMPLETED THE 3 M'S

- [ ] MAKE YOUR BED.
- [ ] MOVE YOUR BODY.
- [ ] MANIFEST YOUR GOALS.

DATE ____________________

DAY ___ / 100

Never give up on a dream just because of the time it will take to accomplish it. The time will pass anyway. *Earl Nightingale*

TODAY I AM GRATEFUL FOR...

AND MY WINS WERE...

AND I COMPLETED THE 3 M'S

- [ ] MAKE YOUR BED.
- [ ] MOVE YOUR BODY.
- [ ] MANIFEST YOUR GOALS.

DATE ____________________

DAY ___ / 100

Your work is going to fill a large part of your life, and the only way to be truly satisfied is to do what you believe is great work. And the only way to do great work is to love what you do. If you haven't found it yet, keep looking. Don't settle. As with all matters of the heart, you'll know when you find it.

Steve Jobs

TODAY I AM GRATEFUL FOR...

AND MY WINS WERE...

AND I COMPLETED THE 3 M'S

- [ ] MAKE YOUR BED.
- [ ] MOVE YOUR BODY.
- [ ] MANIFEST YOUR GOALS.

DATE ____________________

DAY ___ / 100

Some luck lies in not getting what you thought you wanted but getting what you have, which once you have got it you may be smart enough to see is what you would have wanted had you known.

Garrison Keillor

TODAY I AM GRATEFUL FOR...

____

____

____

____

____

AND MY WINS WERE...

____

____

____

____

____

AND I COMPLETED THE 3 M'S

- [ ] MAKE YOUR BED.
- [ ] MOVE YOUR BODY.
- [ ] MANIFEST YOUR GOALS.

DATE ____________________

DAY ___ / 100

Keep your face always toward the sunshine – and shadows will fall behind you.

Walt Whitman

TODAY I AM GRATEFUL FOR...

AND MY WINS WERE...

AND I COMPLETED THE 3 M'S

- [ ] MAKE YOUR BED.
- [ ] MOVE YOUR BODY.
- [ ] MANIFEST YOUR GOALS.

DATE ____________________

DAY ___ / 100

Every champion was once a contender that didn't give up. *Gabby Douglas*

TODAY I AM GRATEFUL FOR...

AND MY WINS WERE...

AND I COMPLETED THE 3 M'S

- [ ] MAKE YOUR BED.
- [ ] MOVE YOUR BODY.
- [ ] MANIFEST YOUR GOALS.

Gratitude

IS THE HEALTHIEST OF ALL HUMAN EMOTIONS. THE MORE YOU EXPRESS GRATITUDE FOR WHAT YOU HAVE, THE MORE LIKELY YOU WILL HAVE EVEN MORE TO EXPRESS GRATITUDE FOR.

ZIG *Ziglar*

Let's Reflect

The past 20 days, I am most proud of...

I want to be more intentional about...

I am going to keep going because...

DATE ____________________

DAY ___ / 100

Success is liking yourself, liking what you do, and liking how you do it.

Maya Angelou

TODAY I AM GRATEFUL FOR...

AND MY WINS WERE...

AND I COMPLETED THE 3 M'S

☐ MAKE YOUR BED. ☐ MOVE YOUR BODY. ☐ MANIFEST YOUR GOALS.

DATE ____________________

DAY ___ / 100

I never lose. Either I win or learn.

Nelson Mandela

TODAY I AM GRATEFUL FOR...

AND MY WINS WERE...

AND I COMPLETED THE 3 M'S

- [ ] MAKE YOUR BED.
- [ ] MOVE YOUR BODY.
- [ ] MANIFEST YOUR GOALS.

DATE ____________________

DAY ___ / 100

Today is your opportunity to build the tomorrow you want.

Ken Poirot

TODAY I AM GRATEFUL FOR...

AND MY WINS WERE...

AND I COMPLETED THE 3 M'S

- [ ] MAKE YOUR BED.
- [ ] MOVE YOUR BODY.
- [ ] MANIFEST YOUR GOALS.

DATE ______________________

DAY ____ / 100

If you want to fly give up everything that weighs you down. *Buddha*

TODAY I AM GRATEFUL FOR...

AND MY WINS WERE...

AND I COMPLETED THE 3 M'S

- [ ] MAKE YOUR BED.
- [ ] MOVE YOUR BODY.
- [ ] MANIFEST YOUR GOALS.

DATE ____________

DAY ___ / 100

You don't need to see the whole staircase, just take the first step.

Martin Luther King Jr.

TODAY I AM GRATEFUL FOR...

AND MY WINS WERE...

AND I COMPLETED THE 3 M'S

- [ ] MAKE YOUR BED.
- [ ] MOVE YOUR BODY.
- [ ] MANIFEST YOUR GOALS.

DATE ____________________

DAY ____ / 100

Twenty years from now you'll be more disappointed by the things you did not do than the ones you did. *Mark Twain*

TODAY I AM GRATEFUL FOR...

AND MY WINS WERE...

AND I COMPLETED THE 3 M'S

☐ MAKE YOUR BED. ☐ MOVE YOUR BODY. ☐ MANIFEST YOUR GOALS.

DATE ____________________

DAY ____ / 100

The world is full of nice people. If you can't find one, be one. *Nishan Panwar*

TODAY I AM GRATEFUL FOR...

AND MY WINS WERE...

AND I COMPLETED THE 3 M'S

- [ ] MAKE YOUR BED.
- [ ] MOVE YOUR BODY.
- [ ] MANIFEST YOUR GOALS.

DATE ____________________

DAY ___ / 100

You can't go back and change the beginning, but you can start where you are and change the ending. *C.S. Lewis*

TODAY I AM GRATEFUL FOR...

____

____

____

____

____

AND MY WINS WERE...

____

____

____

____

____

AND I COMPLETED THE 3 M'S

- [ ] MAKE YOUR BED.
- [ ] MOVE YOUR BODY.
- [ ] MANIFEST YOUR GOALS.

DATE ____________________

DAY ___ / 100

Yesterday I was clever, so I wanted to change the world. Today I am wise, so I am changing myself. *Rumi*

TODAY I AM GRATEFUL FOR...

AND MY WINS WERE...

AND I COMPLETED THE 3 M'S

- [ ] MAKE YOUR BED.
- [ ] MOVE YOUR BODY.
- [ ] MANIFEST YOUR GOALS.

DATE ____________________

DAY ___ / 100

Try not to become a man of success, but rather become a man of value.

Albert Einstein

TODAY I AM GRATEFUL FOR...

AND MY WINS WERE...

AND I COMPLETED THE 3 M'S

☐ MAKE YOUR BED. ☐ MOVE YOUR BODY. ☐ MANIFEST YOUR GOALS.

DATE ____________________

DAY ____ / 100

The world is changed by your example, not by your opinion. *Paulo Coelho*

TODAY I AM GRATEFUL FOR...

AND MY WINS WERE...

AND I COMPLETED THE 3 M'S

- [ ] MAKE YOUR BED.
- [ ] MOVE YOUR BODY.
- [ ] MANIFEST YOUR GOALS.

DATE ____________________

DAY ___ / 100

The best way to predict your future is to create it. *Abraham Lincoln*

TODAY I AM GRATEFUL FOR...

AND MY WINS WERE...

AND I COMPLETED THE 3 M'S

- [ ] MAKE YOUR BED.
- [ ] MOVE YOUR BODY.
- [ ] MANIFEST YOUR GOALS.

DATE ____________________

DAY ____ / 100

Success isn't always about greatness. It's about consistency. Consistent hard work leads to success. Greatness will come.

Dwayne Johnson

TODAY I AM GRATEFUL FOR...

AND MY WINS WERE...

AND I COMPLETED THE 3 M'S

- [ ] MAKE YOUR BED.
- [ ] MOVE YOUR BODY.
- [ ] MANIFEST YOUR GOALS.

DATE ____________________

DAY ___ / 100

If you talk about it, it's a dream. If you envision it, it's possible. If you schedule it, it's real. *Tony Robbins*

TODAY I AM GRATEFUL FOR...

AND MY WINS WERE...

AND I COMPLETED THE 3 M'S

- [ ] MAKE YOUR BED.
- [ ] MOVE YOUR BODY.
- [ ] MANIFEST YOUR GOALS.

DATE ____________________

DAY ___ / 100

Our greatest glory is not in never falling, but in rising every time we fall. *Confucius*

TODAY I AM GRATEFUL FOR...

AND MY WINS WERE...

AND I COMPLETED THE 3 M'S

☐ MAKE YOUR BED. ☐ MOVE YOUR BODY. ☐ MANIFEST YOUR GOALS.

DATE ____________________

DAY ___ / 100

Life is like riding a bicycle. To keep your balance, you must keep moving.

Albert Einstein

TODAY I AM GRATEFUL FOR...

AND MY WINS WERE...

AND I COMPLETED THE 3 M'S

- [ ] MAKE YOUR BED.
- [ ] MOVE YOUR BODY.
- [ ] MANIFEST YOUR GOALS.

DATE ____________

DAY ___ / 100

Never regret a day in your life. Good days bring you happiness and bad days give you experience. *Unknown*

TODAY I AM GRATEFUL FOR...

____

____

____

____

____

AND MY WINS WERE...

____

____

____

____

____

AND I COMPLETED THE 3 M'S

- [ ] MAKE YOUR BED.
- [ ] MOVE YOUR BODY.
- [ ] MANIFEST YOUR GOALS.

DATE ____________

DAY ___ / 100

Life is 10% what happens to you and 90% how you react to it.

Charles R. Swindoll

TODAY I AM GRATEFUL FOR...

AND MY WINS WERE...

AND I COMPLETED THE 3 M'S

- [ ] MAKE YOUR BED.
- [ ] MOVE YOUR BODY.
- [ ] MANIFEST YOUR GOALS.

DATE ____________________

DAY ___ / 100

Very little is needed to make a happy life; it is all within yourself, in your way of thinking. *Marcus Aurelius*

TODAY I AM GRATEFUL FOR...

AND MY WINS WERE...

AND I COMPLETED THE 3 M'S

☐ MAKE YOUR BED. ☐ MOVE YOUR BODY. ☐ MANIFEST YOUR GOALS.

DATE ____________________

DAY ___ / 100

Life's like a movie, write your own ending. Keep believing, keep pretending.

Jim Hensen

TODAY I AM GRATEFUL FOR...

____

____

____

____

____

AND MY WINS WERE...

____

____

____

____

____

AND I COMPLETED THE 3 M'S

☐ MAKE YOUR BED. ☐ MOVE YOUR BODY. ☐ MANIFEST YOUR GOALS.

THE TWO MOST IMPORTANT DAYS IN YOUR LIFE ARE THE DAY YOU'RE BORN AND THE DAY YOU FIND OUT

Why.

MARK *Twain*

Let's Reflect

The past 20 days, I am most proud of...

I want to be more intentional about...

I am going to keep going because...

DATE ____________________

DAY ___ / 100

Do something today that your future self will thank you for. *Unknown*

TODAY I AM GRATEFUL FOR...

AND MY WINS WERE...

AND I COMPLETED THE 3 M'S

☐ MAKE YOUR BED. ☐ MOVE YOUR BODY. ☐ MANIFEST YOUR GOALS.

DATE ____________

DAY ___ / 100

The secret of your future is hidden in your daily routine. *Mike Murdock*

TODAY I AM GRATEFUL FOR...

AND MY WINS WERE...

AND I COMPLETED THE 3 M'S

- [ ] MAKE YOUR BED.
- [ ] MOVE YOUR BODY.
- [ ] MANIFEST YOUR GOALS.

DATE ______________

DAY ___ / 100

Motivation may be what starts you off, but it's habit that keeps you going back for more. *Miya Yamanouchi*

TODAY I AM GRATEFUL FOR...

AND MY WINS WERE...

AND I COMPLETED THE 3 M'S

☐ MAKE YOUR BED. ☐ MOVE YOUR BODY. ☐ MANIFEST YOUR GOALS.

DATE ____________________

DAY ___ / 100

As we express our gratitude, we must never forget that the highest form of appreciation is not to utter words, but to live by them.

John F. Kennedy

TODAY I AM GRATEFUL FOR...

AND MY WINS WERE...

AND I COMPLETED THE 3 M'S

- [ ] MAKE YOUR BED.
- [ ] MOVE YOUR BODY.
- [ ] MANIFEST YOUR GOALS.

DATE ____________________

DAY ___ / 100

It is never too late to be what you might have been. *George Eliot*

TODAY I AM GRATEFUL FOR...

AND MY WINS WERE...

AND I COMPLETED THE 3 M'S

- [ ] MAKE YOUR BED.
- [ ] MOVE YOUR BODY.
- [ ] MANIFEST YOUR GOALS.

DATE ____________________

DAY ___ / 100

Strength doesn't come from what you can do. It comes from overcoming the things you once thought you couldn't.

Rikki Rogers

TODAY I AM GRATEFUL FOR...

AND MY WINS WERE...

AND I COMPLETED THE 3 M'S

- [ ] MAKE YOUR BED.
- [ ] MOVE YOUR BODY.
- [ ] MANIFEST YOUR GOALS.

DATE ____________________

DAY ___ / 100

So often in life, things that you regard as an impediment turn out to be great, good fortune. *Ruth Bader Ginsburg*

TODAY I AM GRATEFUL FOR...

AND MY WINS WERE...

AND I COMPLETED THE 3 M'S

☐ MAKE YOUR BED. ☐ MOVE YOUR BODY. ☐ MANIFEST YOUR GOALS.

DATE ____________________

DAY ___ / 100

The happiest people don't have the best of everything, they just make the best of everything. *Unknown*

TODAY I AM GRATEFUL FOR...

AND MY WINS WERE...

AND I COMPLETED THE 3 M'S

- [ ] MAKE YOUR BED.
- [ ] MOVE YOUR BODY.
- [ ] MANIFEST YOUR GOALS.

DATE ______________

DAY ___ / 100

What we know matters but who we are matters more. *Brene Brown*

TODAY I AM GRATEFUL FOR...

AND MY WINS WERE...

AND I COMPLETED THE 3 M'S

☐ MAKE YOUR BED. ☐ MOVE YOUR BODY. ☐ MANIFEST YOUR GOALS.

DATE ____________________

DAY ___ / 100

Be yourself, but always your better self.

Karl G. Maeser

TODAY I AM GRATEFUL FOR...

AND MY WINS WERE...

AND I COMPLETED THE 3 M'S

- [ ] MAKE YOUR BED.
- [ ] MOVE YOUR BODY.
- [ ] MANIFEST YOUR GOALS.

DATE ____________

DAY ___ / 100

Wherever you go, go with all your heart.

Confucius

TODAY I AM GRATEFUL FOR...

AND MY WINS WERE...

AND I COMPLETED THE 3 M'S

- [ ] MAKE YOUR BED.
- [ ] MOVE YOUR BODY.
- [ ] MANIFEST YOUR GOALS.

DATE ______________

DAY ___ / 100

Show up every single day, don't worry about what others have to say and don't let the fear of what might happen keep you from at least trying.

Adriana Carrig

TODAY I AM GRATEFUL FOR...

AND MY WINS WERE...

AND I COMPLETED THE 3 M'S

☐ MAKE YOUR BED. ☐ MOVE YOUR BODY. ☐ MANIFEST YOUR GOALS.

DATE ____________________

DAY ___ / 100

The secret isn't really a secret, it's more of the determination that you refuse to settle for anything less than your best again.

Sarah Geer

TODAY I AM GRATEFUL FOR...

AND MY WINS WERE...

AND I COMPLETED THE 3 M'S

- [ ] MAKE YOUR BED.
- [ ] MOVE YOUR BODY.
- [ ] MANIFEST YOUR GOALS.

DATE ____________________

DAY ___ / 100

If you want to change the world, go home and love your family. *Mother Teresa*

TODAY I AM GRATEFUL FOR...

AND MY WINS WERE...

AND I COMPLETED THE 3 M'S

- [ ] MAKE YOUR BED.
- [ ] MOVE YOUR BODY.
- [ ] MANIFEST YOUR GOALS.

DATE ____________________

DAY ___ / 100

A winner is a dreamer who never gives up.

Nelson Mandela

TODAY I AM GRATEFUL FOR...

AND MY WINS WERE...

AND I COMPLETED THE 3 M'S

- [ ] MAKE YOUR BED.
- [ ] MOVE YOUR BODY.
- [ ] MANIFEST YOUR GOALS.

DATE ____________________

DAY ___ / 100

Gratitude and attitude are not challenges; they are choices. *Robert Braathe*

TODAY I AM GRATEFUL FOR...

AND MY WINS WERE...

AND I COMPLETED THE 3 M'S

☐ MAKE YOUR BED. ☐ MOVE YOUR BODY. ☐ MANIFEST YOUR GOALS.

DATE ____________________

DAY ___ / 100

If you only say one prayer in a day, make it thank you. *Rumi*

TODAY I AM GRATEFUL FOR...

AND MY WINS WERE...

AND I COMPLETED THE 3 M'S

☐ MAKE YOUR BED. ☐ MOVE YOUR BODY. ☐ MANIFEST YOUR GOALS.

DATE ____________________

DAY ___ / 100

Happiness cannot be traveled to, owned, earned, worn or consumed. Happiness is the spiritual experience of living every minute with love, grace and gratitude.

Deni Waitley

TODAY I AM GRATEFUL FOR...

AND MY WINS WERE...

AND I COMPLETED THE 3 M'S

- [ ] MAKE YOUR BED.
- [ ] MOVE YOUR BODY.
- [ ] MANIFEST YOUR GOALS.

DATE ____________________

DAY ___ / 100

The most powerful weapon against your daily battles is finding the courage to be grateful anyway. *Unknown*

TODAY I AM GRATEFUL FOR...

AND MY WINS WERE...

AND I COMPLETED THE 3 M'S

- [ ] MAKE YOUR BED.
- [ ] MOVE YOUR BODY.
- [ ] MANIFEST YOUR GOALS.

DATE ____________________

DAY ___ / 100

Do not spoil what you have by desiring what you have not; Remember that what you now have was once among the things you only hoped for.

Epicurus

TODAY I AM GRATEFUL FOR...

AND MY WINS WERE...

AND I COMPLETED THE 3 M'S

☐ MAKE YOUR BED. ☐ MOVE YOUR BODY. ☐ MANIFEST YOUR GOALS.

I've learned that whenever I decide something with an open heart, I usually make the right decision. I've learned that even when I have pains, I don't have to be one. I've learned that every day you should reach out and touch someone. People love a warm hug, or just a friendly pat on the back. I've learned that I still have a lot to learn. I've learned that people will forget what you said, people will forget what you did, but people will never forget how you made them feel.

MAYA *Angelou*

Let's Reflect

The past 20 days, I am most proud of...

I want to be more intentional about...

I am going to keep going because...

YOU *did it!*

You finished 100 days of gratitude! You are now an official member of the #100daysofgratitudechallenge club. You are a founding member and you should be so proud of yourself. 90% of people nowadays do not even set aside 10 minutes a day to do something for themselves. Now, YOU, you my friend, you did that. You were intentional and you committed!

What I love about writing down your intentions and the gratitude that you have each day is that you now have this special little home for all the feelings, the happiness, and the things that you were thankful for. It is now in a book that you can hold, feel, and see, and know that your gratitude resides in that place.

SO NOW WHAT?!?!?

You keep going. You didn't come this far just to come this far, right? You started something monumental and something that means something! So you do it all over again. Maybe this time you do it with a friend or a family member. Maybe you get a group together to do another 100 day challenge and inspire more people. Maybe you challenge yourself to add additional gratitude each day or to think of more of a variety of things to be grateful for.

You are in charge here, you can do anything you want!

So now you have some extra space ... I intentionally added a couple pages for a notes section so you can take this time to write down anything you want. Reflect on all of your gratitude, how did you do on your 3 M's, how did you do with writing down your intentions?

Take this note section to write down reminders for yourself or anything you want that will help keep you going and start your next journal!

Thank you for picking up this journal, for trusting the journal, for trusting me, and for going for it. I hope that each day you were inspired and excited to keep going. My vision for this journal was to see other women intentionally using something that I know has helped me become a better person and get more out of life.

My goal has always been to work on being the best version of myself and help others along the way. I hope this journal did that for you.

I hope to see you online, to see you on the various social media platforms, to be tagged in your life's accomplishments, the times you were inspired, the times you inspired others ...

I want you to know that I truly believe that you, the girl who made it to the back of this book, can be anything she wants to be in her life. I want you to leave believing in yourself, going for what you want and sometimes even inspiring yourself.

Though this is the end of the journal, this is not goodbye. I will see you online, I will see you through email, I will always be around, and I hope to one day hear how this journal inspired you.

Let's keep this going, girl!
Let's inspire, together!

XOXO, *Farin*

Made in the USA
Middletown, DE
02 March 2021